I'm Thinking of a Great Plains State

Bela Davis

Abdo Kids Junior
is an Imprint of Abdo Kids
abdobooks.com

abdobooks.com

Published by Abdo Kids, a division of ABDO, P.O. Box 398166, Minneapolis, Minnesota 55439.

Printed in the United States of America, North Mankato, Minnesota.

102025

012026

THIS BOOK CONTAINS RECYCLED MATERIALS

Photo Credits: Getty Images, Shutterstock

Production Contributors: Teddy Borth, Jennie Forsberg, Grace Hansen

Design Contributors: Candice Keimig, Pakou Moua

Library of Congress Control Number: 2025936485

Publisher's Cataloging-in-Publication Data

Names: Davis, Bela, author.

Title: I'm thinking of a great plains state / by Bela Davis

Description: Minneapolis, Minnesota : Abdo Kids, 2026 | Series: I'm thinking of a state | Includes online resources and index.

Identifiers: ISBN 9798384907374 (lib. bdg.) | ISBN 9798384908074 (ebook) | ISBN 9798384908425 (Read-to-Me ebook)

Subjects: LCSH: Great Plains--Juvenile literature. | American states (United States)--Juvenile literature. | Geography--Juvenile literature. | Physical geography--United States--Juvenile literature.

Classification: DDC 917--dc23

Table of Contents

Guess the State!

I'm thinking of a Great Plains state. The Great Plains is in the middle of the United States. It has large areas of mostly flat land.

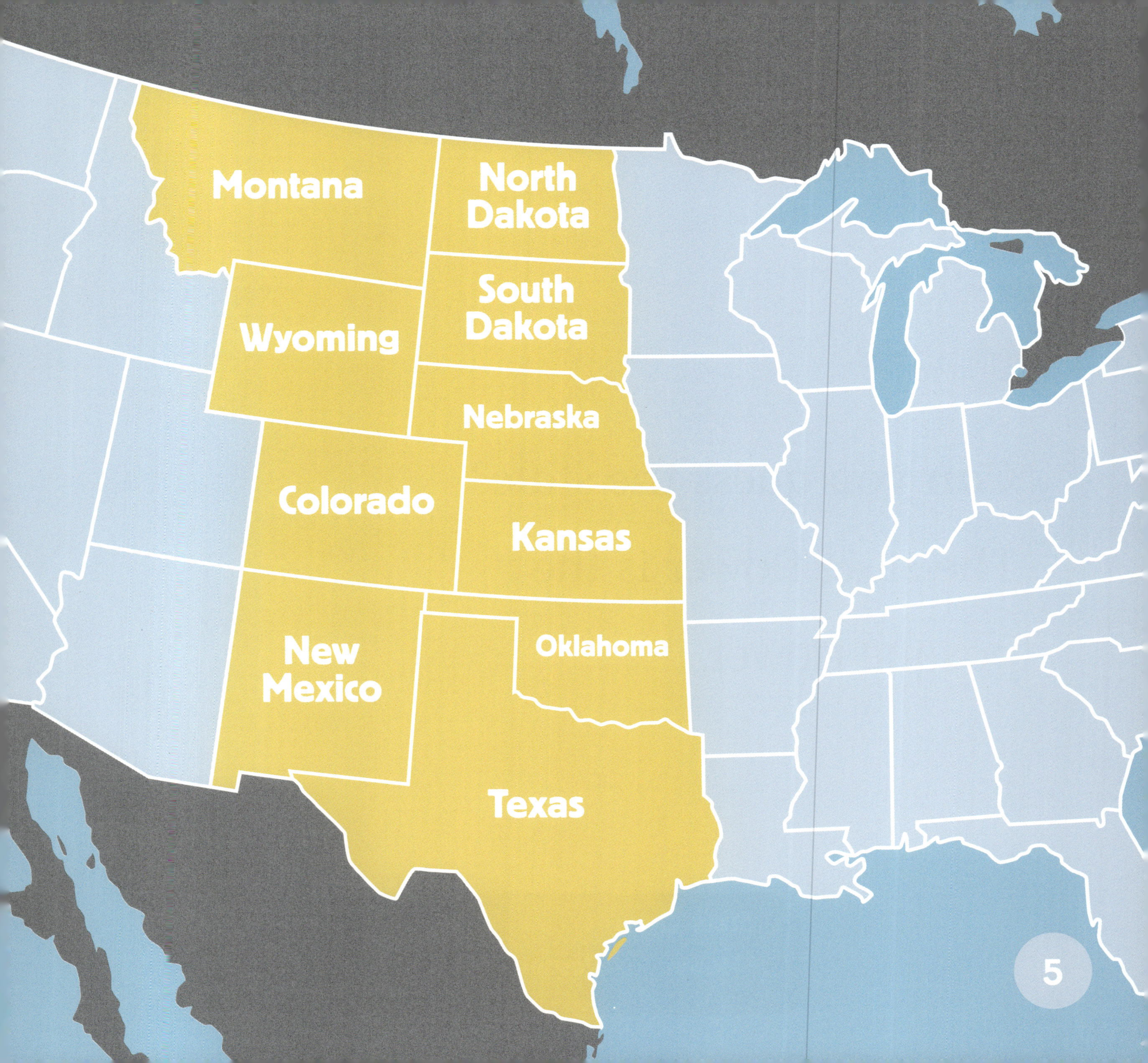
Montana
North Dakota
South Dakota
Wyoming
Nebraska
Colorado
Kansas
New Mexico
Oklahoma
Texas

Can you guess the state?

The state flower is the pasque flower.

State Clues

- **Flower:** Pasque flower

The state bird is the ring-necked pheasant.

State Clues

- **Flower:** Pasque flower
- **Bird:** Ring-necked pheasant

Prairie dogs live in this state.

State Clues

- **Flower:** Pasque flower
- **Bird:** Ring-necked pheasant
- **Animal:** Prairie dog

Woolly mammoth **fossils** have been found here.

State Clues

- **Flower:** Pasque flower
- **Bird:** Ring-necked pheasant
- **Animal:** Prairie dog
- **Activity:** Dig for fossils

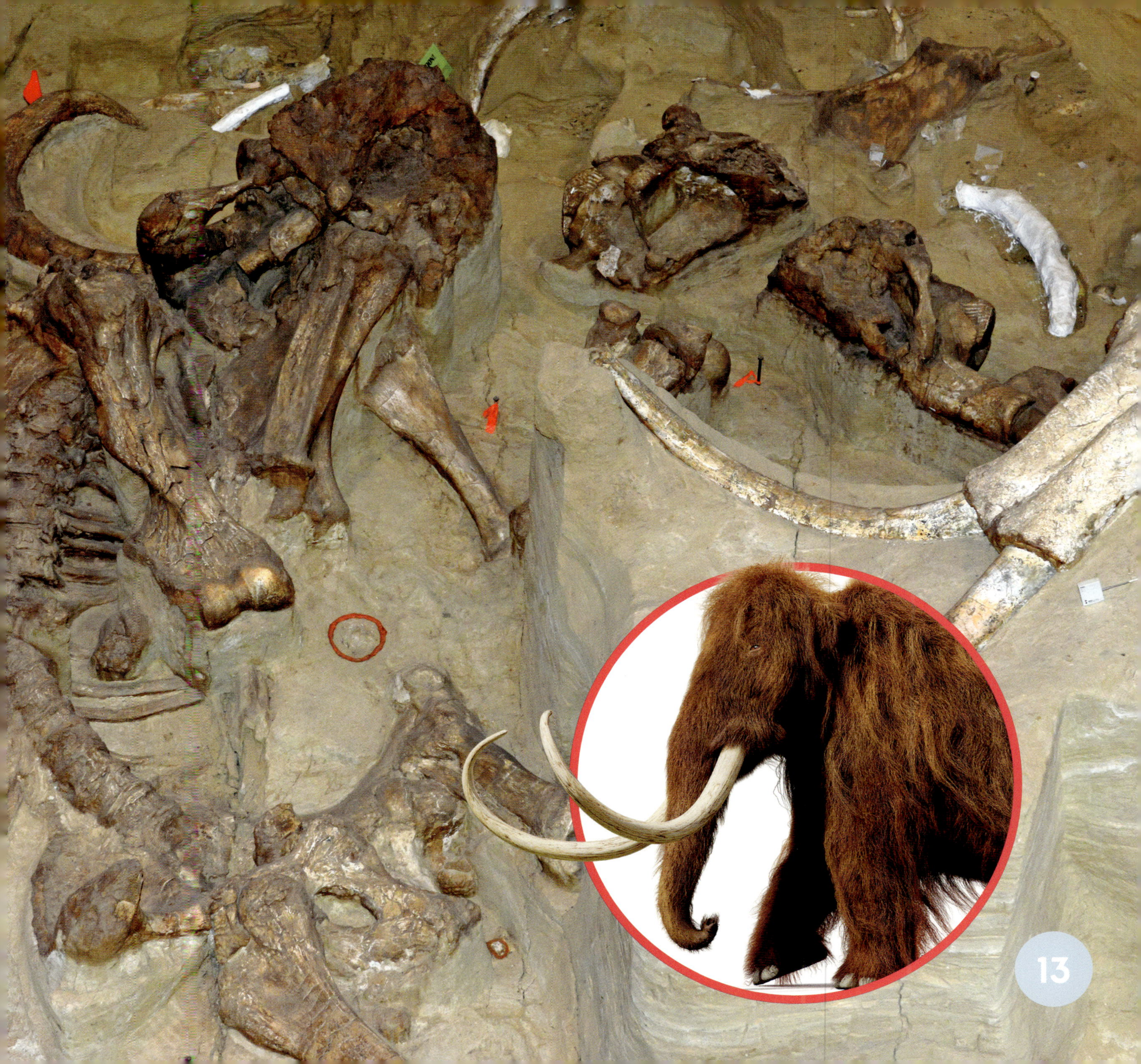

People visit Mount Rushmore in this state.

State Clues

• Flower:	Pasque flower
• Bird:	Ring-necked pheasant
• Animal:	Prairie dog
• Activity:	Dig for fossils
• Visit:	Mount Rushmore

People can explore Badlands National Park in this state.

State Clues

- **Flower:** Pasque flower
- **Bird:** Ring-necked pheasant
- **Animal:** Prairie dog
- **Activity:** Dig for fossils
- **Visit:** Mount Rushmore
- **Explore:** Badlands

The state's capital is Pierre.

State Clues

- **Flower:** Pasque flower
- **Bird:** Ring-necked pheasant
- **Animal:** Prairie dog
- **Activity:** Dig for fossils
- **Visit:** Mount Rushmore
- **Explore:** Badlands
- **Capital:** Pierre

Now you have all the clues! Can you guess what state I'm thinking of?

State Clues

- **Flower:** Pasque flower
- **Bird:** Ring-necked pheasant
- **Animal:** Prairie dog
- **Activity:** Dig for fossils
- **Visit:** Mount Rushmore
- **Explore:** Badlands
- **Capital:** Pierre

MT
ND
WY
SD

I'm Thinking of...

South Dakota!

Glossary

fossil
the remains or trace of a living animal or plant from a long time ago.

national park
a special area of land that is set aside by the United States government to protect it.

Index

Abdo Kids ONLINE

FREE! ONLINE MULTIMEDIA RESOURCES

Visit **abdokids.com** to access crafts, games, videos, and more!

Use Abdo Kids code

IIK7374

or scan this QR code!

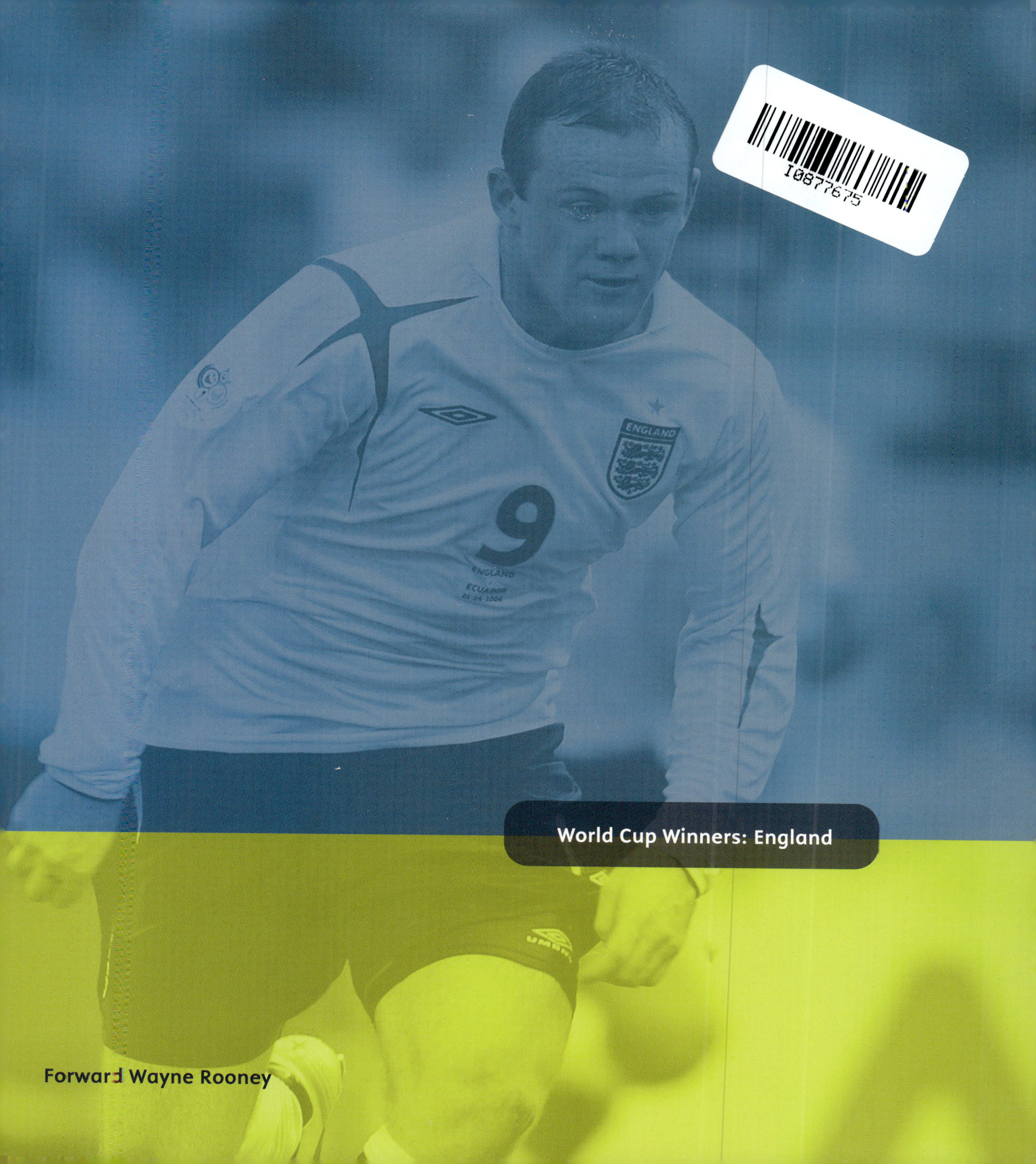

World Cup Winners: England

Forward Wayne Rooney

Striker Alan Shearer

WORLD CUP WINNERS

ENGLAND

JASON OLSON

CREATIVE EDUCATION / CREATIVE PAPERBACKS

Published by Creative Education and Creative Paperbacks
P.O. Box 227, Mankato, Minnesota 56002
Creative Education and Creative Paperbacks are imprints of
The Creative Company
www.thecreativecompany.us

Book design by Blue Design (www.bluedes.com)

Images by Getty Images, Catherine Ivill, 16, Dan Mullan, cover, 7, David Cannon, 15, Don Morley, 19, Hulton Deutsch, 12, Mike King/Allsport, 20, Richard Sellers/Allstar, 2, 3, 10, 24, Stewart Kendall/Allstar, 1, Stu Forster, 5, Sylvain Sonnet, 9; Unsplash/Winston Tjia, 6; Wikimedia Commons/public domain, 4
Every effort has been made to contact copyright holders for material reproduced in this book. Any omissions will be rectified in subsequent printings if notice is given to the publisher.

Library of Congress Cataloging-in-Publication Data
Names: Olson, Jason, 1981– author.
Title: England / Jason Olson.
Description: Mankato, Minnesota : Creative Education and Creative Paperbacks, 2026. | Series: Creative sports. World Cup winners | Includes index. | Audience: Ages 7-10 | Audience: Grades 2-3 | Summary: "England is the birthplace of soccer, and it won the FIFA World Cup in 1966. This elementary title follows the "Three Lions" through thrilling soccer action as they seek another world soccer title"– Provided by publisher.
Identifiers: LCCN 2024046132 (print) | LCCN 2024046133 (ebook) | ISBN 9798889896005 (library binding) | ISBN 9781682777664 (paperback) | ISBN 9798889896807 (ebook)
Subjects: LCSH: Soccer–England–History–Juvenile literature. | World Cup (Soccer)–History–Juvenile literature.
Classification: LCC GV944.G7 057 2026 (print) | LCC GV944.G7 (ebook) | DDC 796.3340942–dc23/eng/20241212
LC record available at https://lccn.loc.gov/2024046132
LC ebook record available at https://lccn.loc.gov/2024046133

Printed in India

Attacking midfielder Paul Gascoigne

The Three Lions badge

CONTENTS

Home of the Team

England is part of the United Kingdom—along with Scotland, Wales, and Northern Ireland. Its capital London is one of the world's greatest cities.

The English love soccer, and for good reason. Their national team is one of the few teams to have won the World Cup. The World Cup is a worldwide soccer tournament. Countries make teams of their best players. Every four years, they compete to become world champion.

Waterloo 211
abellio

Midfielder David Beckham

Team Traditions

The England national team is known as "The Three Lions" for the three lions on its jersey. The lions were the crest of King Richard I, called the Lionheart.

England plays "route one" soccer. This style relies on long, high passes to get the ball to the opponent's goal fast. England's main **rivals** are Scotland, Germany, and Argentina.

Centre-back Bobby Moore

Team History

The first rules of modern soccer were made in England in 1863. England and Scotland played to a 0–0 draw in the first international match in 1872.

England first played in the World Cup in 1950. In 1966, it won its only World Cup as host. In the final, England beat West Germany 4–2 in extra time. Geoff Hurst scored a **hat trick**. The win sent the nation into a huge celebration. Captain Bobby Moore accepted the trophy from Queen Elizabeth II after the final.

West Germany knocked England out of the quarterfinals in 1970. The West Germans were behind 2–0. But they came back to win 3–2. The "Hand of God" and "Goal of the Century" goals helped Argentina defeat England 2–1 in the 1986 quarterfinals. West Germany topped England 4–3 in a penalty shootout in the 1990 semifinals.

Argentina vs. England, 1986

Striker Harry Kane

Gareth Southgate became manager in 2016. The team reached the 2018 World Cup semifinals, but lost to Croatia 2–1 in extra time. England's star striker Harry Kane was the top scorer in the tournament. He scored six goals to earn the **Golden Boot**.

Team Stars

England has had many great stars in its history. Sir Bobby Charlton is known for his long-range shooting with either foot. He scored 49 times in 106 games. Charlton rarely broke the rules and received only two yellow cards in his whole career. He won the **Ballon d'Or** and the **Golden Ball** in 1966. Bobby Moore is one of the best defenders of all time. He played 108 matches for England.

Midfielder Bobby Charlton

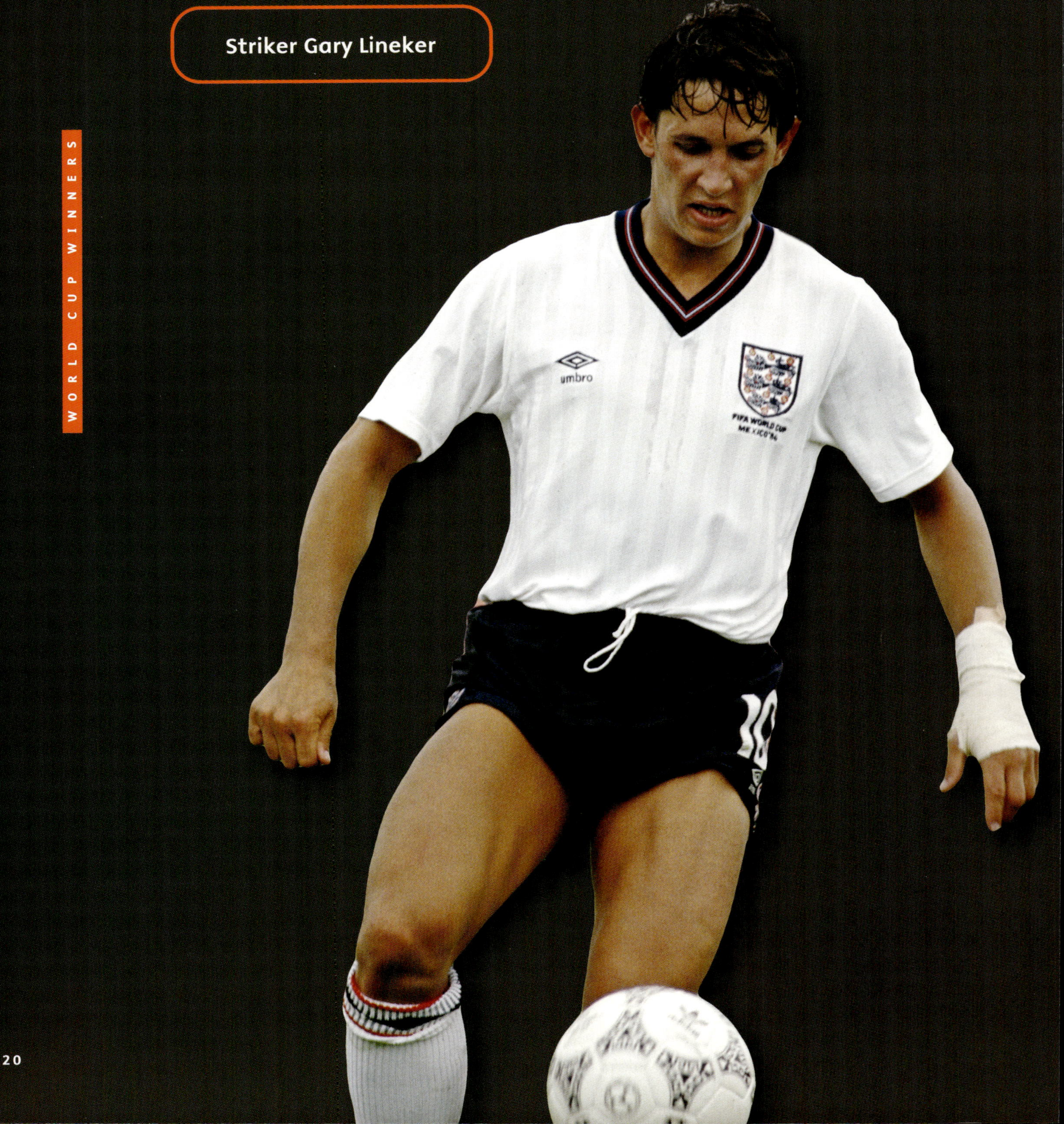

Striker Gary Lineker

Gary Lineker holds the team record for goals in World Cup matches, with 10 goals. Goalkeeper Peter Shilton holds the **caps** record, with 125 matches over 20 years of play. Kane is at the top of the recent list, with 66 goals in 98 matches. Jude Bellingham and other young players hope to bring another World Cup to England soon.

About the England National Team

First year: 1872

Team colors: white, red, navy, black

Home stadium: Wembley Stadium

WORLD CUP VICTORY:

1966, 4–2 over West Germany

WEBSITE

https://www.englandfootball.com/

Glossary

Ballon d'Or — an award given every year to the world's best soccer player

cap — an official match played for a national soccer team

Golden Ball — an award given to the best player in the World Cup

Golden Boot — an award given to the player with the most goals in a tournament

hat trick — when a player scores three goals in a single match

rival — a team that plays extra hard against another team

Midfielders Jude Bellingham (left) and Conor Gallagher (right)

Index